4.7
0.5

#170589

W9-AAD-696

WITHDRAWN

PUBLIC LIBRARY
DANVILLE, ILLINOIS

# COMPARING ANIMAL TRAITS

# VAMPIRE BATS
## NIGHTTIME FLYING MAMMALS

REBECCA E. HIRSCH

Lerner Publications ◆ Minneapolis

Copyright © 2015 by Lerner Publishing Group, Inc.

All rights reserved. International copyright secured. No part of this book may be reproduced, stored in a retrieval system, or transmitted in any form or by any means—electronic, mechanical, photocopying, recording, or otherwise—without the prior written permission of Lerner Publishing Group, Inc., except for the inclusion of brief quotations in an acknowledged review.

Lerner Publications Company
A division of Lerner Publishing Group, Inc.
241 First Avenue North
Minneapolis, MN 55401 USA

For reading levels and more information, look up this title at www.lernerbooks.com.


Photo Acknowledgments

The images in this book are used with the permission of: © Barry Mansell/naturepl.com, pp. 1, 5; © Nick Gordon/ardea.com, p. 4; Dr. Brock Felton/National Science Foundation, p. 6; © Oxford Scientific/Getty Images, p. 7 (top); © Bruce Dale/National Geographic/Getty Images, p. 7 (bottom); © Vincent St. Thomas/Shutterstock.com, p. 8; © Timothy Laman/National Geographic/Getty Images, p. 9 (top); Haroldo Palo Jr./NHPA/Photoshot/Newscom, p. 9 (bottom left); Nick Garbutt/NHPA/Photoshot/Newscom, p. 9 (bottom right); © iStockphoto.com/mikeuk, p. 10; © Chriswood44/Dreamstime.com, p. 11 (bottom right); Michael & Patricia Fogden/Minden Pictures/Newscom, p. 11 (bottom left); © Mapping Specialists, Ltd., Madison, WI, p. 12; © Ben Lascelles/naturepl.com, p. 13; © Minden Pictures/SuperStock, pp. 14, 17 (bottom right); Pete Oxford/Minden Pictures/Newscom, p. 15 (top); © Pete Oxford/naturepl.com, p. 15 (bottom); © outdoorsman/Shutterstock.com, p. 16; © Dietmar Nill/Nature Picture Library/CORBIS, p. 17 (bottom left); © Victor Habbick Visions/Science Source, p. 18; © Zigmund Leszczynski/Animals Animals, p. 19; Norbert Wu/Minden Pictures/Newscom, pp. 20, 21 (top); © Carsten Peter/National Geographic/Getty Images, p. 21 (bottom left); © iStockphoto.com/CoreyFord, p. 21 (bottom right); © Stephen J Krasemann/All Canada Photos/SuperStock, p. 22; © JIM CLARE/naturepl.com, p. 23 (bottom left); © Leonard Lee Rue III/Photo Researchers/Getty Images, p. 23 (bottom right); AP Photo/JAKE SCHOELLKOPF, p. 24; © B. G. Thomson/Science Source, p. 25; © Frans Lanting/CORBIS, p. 26; © iStockphoto.com/Enjoylife2, p. 27; BILL GREENBLATT/UPI/Newscom, p. 28.

Front cover: Stephen Dalton/NHPA/Photoshot/Newscom.
Back cover: © belizar/Shutterstock.com.

Main body text set in Calvert MT Std 12/18. Typeface provided by Monotype Typography.


Library of Congress Cataloging-in-Publication Data

Hirsch, Rebecca E., author.
    Vampire bats : nighttime flying mammals / by Rebecca E. Hirsch.
        pages    cm. — (Comparing animal traits)
    Summary: "This book covers information (life cycle, appearance, habitat) about the vampire bat. Each chapter discusses an aspect of the vampire bat's life, comparing the bat to a similar mammal and to a very different mammal."—Provided by publisher.
    Includes index.
    ISBN 978-1-4677-5879-6 (lib. bdg. : alk. paper)
    ISBN 978-1-4677-6066-9 (pbk.)
    ISBN 978-1-4677-6222-9 (EB pdf)
    1. Vampire bats—Behavior—Juvenile literature. 2. Vampire bats—Life cycles—Juvenile literature. 3. Vampire bats—Juvenile literature. I. Title.
    QL737.C52H57 2015
    599.4'5—dc23

2014022618

Manufactured in the United States of America
1 — BP —12/31/14

79.45
HIR
cop.1

# TABLE OF CONTENTS

PUBLIC LIBRARY
DANVILLE, ILLINOIS

# MEET THE VAMPIRE BAT

**A vampire bat glides low over the ground.** The bat lands next to a sleeping cow. The vampire bat hops forward and makes a tiny cut on the cow's hoof. The cow's blood flows, and the bat feasts. Vampire bats are mammals, a kind of animal. Other kinds of animals include insects, fish, amphibians, reptiles, and birds.

Vampire bats drink the blood of other animals.

Mammals share certain traits. All mammals are vertebrates, animals with backbones. All mammals are also warm-blooded. Their bodies stay warm even in cold temperatures. All mammals have hair or fur. All female mammals feed their babies milk.

Vampire bats share these and other traits with other mammals. They also have traits that set them apart. Vampire bats can fly. And vampire bats are the only mammals that can survive on blood alone.

Unlike many other mammals, vampire bats have wings.

# CHAPTER 1

# WHAT DO VAMPIRE BATS LOOK LIKE?

**Common vampire bats are small animals with pointed ears and grayish-brown fur.** You can find them hanging upside down in caves. With its wings folded, the vampire bat is not much bigger than your thumb. When the bat flies, its wingspan is as long as an unsharpened pencil.

Skin stretches over the vampire bat's arm bones and finger bones to form wings. To fly, the bat flaps its wings up and down. It moves its fingers to expand its wings and to change its speed

Vampire bats can fold and unfold their wings.

In addition to wings, vampire bats have strong back legs.

or direction. A thumb claw pokes out of each wing. With its thumb claws and its strong back legs, a vampire bat can walk, run, and hop on the ground.

The vampire bat uses two pointy front teeth to cut the skin of its prey. The bat's saliva prevents the host animal's blood from clotting (becoming a solid). That way, the bat can drink its fill. Rather than sucking blood from the cut, the bat laps up blood with its tongue.

**DID YOU KNOW?**
**Three species of bats live on BLOOD. In addition to the common vampire bat, those species are the hairy-legged vampire bat and the white-winged vampire bat.**

# VAMPIRE BATS VS. COLUGOS

Colugos sail through trees in the jungles of Asia. These cat-sized mammals hang from branches by their sharp claws. Although colugos are bigger than vampire bats, the two animals look alike in many ways. Both have furry bodies and big eyes, and both like to hang upside down.

Colugos and vampire bats have bodies adapted for air travel. Vampire bats have wings. Colugos have a flap of skin called a patagium. This flap stretches from the side of the neck to the tips of the limbs to the end of the colugo's tail. When the colugo spreads its legs wide, it looks like a kite.

Colugos use claws for hanging and climbing.

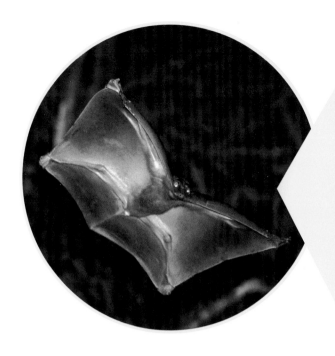

**DID YOU KNOW?**
In a single leap, a colugo can **GLIDE** 110 yards (100 meters) or more. That's nearly the length of a football field.

Vampire bats fly by flapping their wings. Colugos glide on air currents. Using their flaps like parachutes, these mammals sail from one tree to another. Scientists think the ancestors of vampire bats may have first taken to the air by gliding the way colugos do.

Both vampire bats (*left*) and colugos (*right*) like to hang upside down.

# VAMPIRE BATS VS. WALRUSES

Walruses splash through icy waters. These mammals live in noisy herds near the North Pole. Walruses are much larger than vampire bats. A vampire bat weighs less than a golf ball. A walrus can weigh as much as a car.

Thick fur covers the body of a vampire bat. A walrus looks hairless. The hair it does have is thin. A walrus also has a mustache of whiskers. Vampire bats have leathery wings. Walruses have flippers. The flippers are square-shaped in front and triangle-shaped in back. Walruses can walk on the ice on all four flippers. In the water, they use their flippers to paddle and steer.

Even the teeth of vampire bats and walruses differ. Vampire bats have tiny, sharp teeth. Walruses have rounded teeth. Two of the teeth grow into long tusks. Walruses dig their tusks into the ice to pull their bulky bodies out of the water. They also use the tusks to fight off **predators**.

A walrus's body is big and bulky, but walruses can still move smoothly through water.

# COMPARE IT!

**VAMPIRE BATS**

VS.

**WALRUSES**

| | HEAD AND BODY LENGTH | |
|---|---|---|
| **2.5 TO 3.5 INCHES** (6.3 TO 8.9 CENTIMETERS) | | **8.2 TO 10.5 FEET** (2.5 TO 3.2 M) |

| | WEIGHT | |
|---|---|---|
| **0.5 TO 1.5 OUNCES** (14 TO 43 GRAMS) | | **565 TO 3,000 POUNDS** (256 TO 1,360 KILOGRAMS) |

| | FRONT TEETH | |
|---|---|---|
| V-shaped | | Long and pointed |

# CHAPTER 2

# WHERE DO VAMPIRE BATS LIVE?

**Vampire bats fly through the night across Mexico, Central America,** and South America. They live in tropical forests and deserts. Although they are warm-blooded, vampire bats cannot survive outside warm climates. Vampire bats are also nocturnal (active at night).

NORTH AMERICA

ATLANTIC OCEAN

PACIFIC OCEAN

SOUTH AMERICA

N
W — E
S

Vampire bat habitat

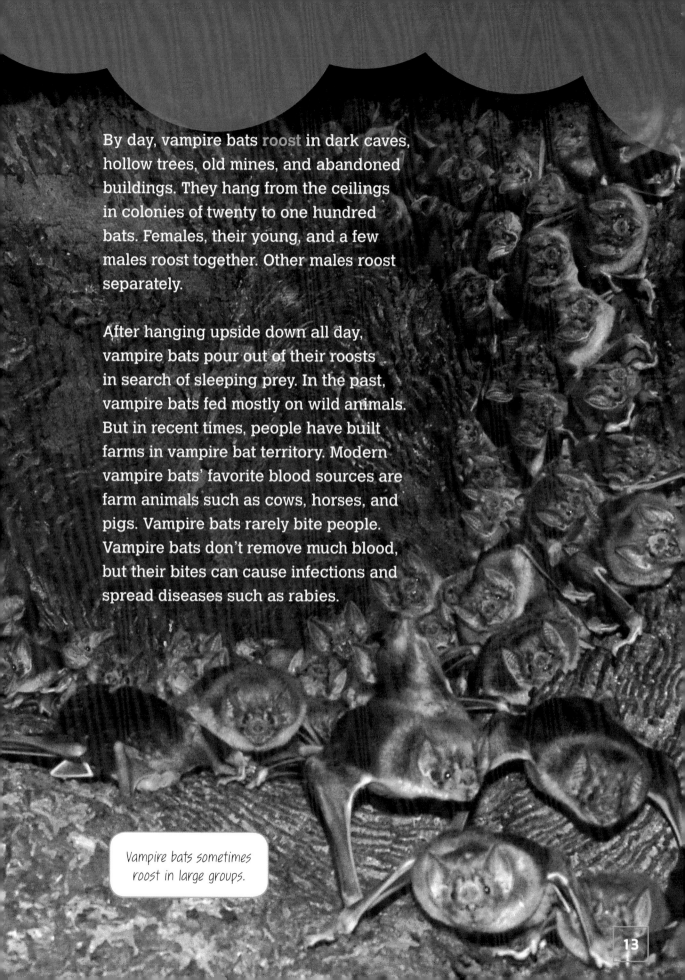

By day, vampire bats roost in dark caves, hollow trees, old mines, and abandoned buildings. They hang from the ceilings in colonies of twenty to one hundred bats. Females, their young, and a few males roost together. Other males roost separately.

After hanging upside down all day, vampire bats pour out of their roosts in search of sleeping prey. In the past, vampire bats fed mostly on wild animals. But in recent times, people have built farms in vampire bat territory. Modern vampire bats' favorite blood sources are farm animals such as cows, horses, and pigs. Vampire bats rarely bite people. Vampire bats don't remove much blood, but their bites can cause infections and spread diseases such as rabies.

Vampire bats sometimes roost in large groups.

# VAMPIRE BATS VS. WHITE-LIPPED PECCARIES

White-lipped peccaries root through forests in Mexico, Central America, and South America. These piglike mammals forage for fruit, leaves, mushrooms, insects, and turtle eggs. Although white-lipped peccaries and vampire bats eat different foods, they live in similar habitats. Both vampire bats and white-lipped peccaries inhabit tropical forests as well as drier parts of the tropics.

The body of a white-lipped peccary is adapted for life in the tropics.

**DID YOU KNOW?**
Vampire bats get plenty of **WATER** from their liquid diet. But peccaries rarely stray too far from bodies of water.

Both white-lipped peccaries and vampire bats take shelter during the day. Like vampire bats, peccaries often rest in caves. You might also find them snoozing under large boulders and in thickets. And like vampire bats, peccaries search for food at night. Peccary herds roam through larger areas to find enough to eat. They sometimes raid farm fields for corn, sweet potatoes, sugarcane, and bananas.

Like vampire bats, white-lipped peccaries often find shelter inside caves.

# VAMPIRE BATS VS. POLAR BEARS

Polar bears lumber across the ice in northern parts of the world. Like vampire bats, polar bears are predators, but these mammals live in different habitats. Vampire bats stay in warm areas, but polar bears love the cold. These powerful mammals are adapted to survive in the Arctic, one of the coldest places on Earth.

Vampire bats live and hunt in one area. But polar bears wander their Arctic habitat in search of floating sea ice. They use this ice as a platform for hunting seals. A polar bear might walk or swim long distances as the sea ice melts and freezes through the year.

While vampire bats sleep in caves and other enclosed spaces, polar bears don't need much shelter. Polar bears usually sleep in the open. Other predators avoid the bear because of its strength and size. The bear's warm fur and thick blubber keep it warm in even the coldest weather. If a snowstorm hits, a polar bear digs a resting spot in the snow, lies down, and waits for the storm to pass.

# COMPARE IT!

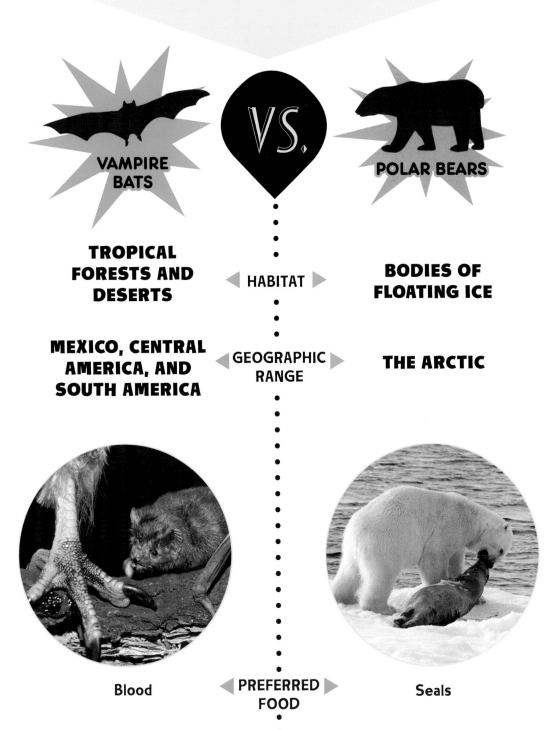

VAMPIRE BATS **VS.** POLAR BEARS

| | | |
|---|---|---|
| TROPICAL FORESTS AND DESERTS | ◀ HABITAT ▶ | BODIES OF FLOATING ICE |
| MEXICO, CENTRAL AMERICA, AND SOUTH AMERICA | ◀ GEOGRAPHIC RANGE ▶ | THE ARCTIC |
| Blood | ◀ PREFERRED FOOD ▶ | Seals |

# CHAPTER 3

# THE NIGHT HUNT OF VAMPIRE BATS

**Vampire bats wait for the darkest part of the night and then fly silently out of caves and hollow trees.** They find their way using echolocation. A bat makes a high-pitched chirp that pulses through the air. When the sound hits an object, the sound bounces back. From the echo, the bat can learn an object's size, shape, and location.

The circles in this diagram illustrate the chirp of a vampire bat. The bat's chirp travels out into the night and then bounces back toward the bat.

**DID YOU KNOW?**
Vampire bats can **DOUBLE** their weight after a meal. Sometimes they are too heavy to take off after eating!

The vampire bat lands near its sleeping prey. The bat gently hops onto the animal. Heat sensors in the bat's nose reveal a feeding spot on the skin of the prey. The warmest spot has the most blood underneath it. If the host animal wakes, the bat leaps out of harm's way.

Vampire bats share food. One bat needs only about 2 tablespoons (30 milliliters) of blood each day. But vampire bats cannot always find food, and a hungry bat can starve in just two days. So roost-mates sometimes regurgitate their meals. A bat brings swallowed blood back up into its mouth. Other hungry bats can drink this blood.

# VAMPIRE BATS VS.
# SPERM WHALES

Sperm whales swim in all the oceans of the world. These mammals search for squid, fish, and octopuses to eat. The school-bus-sized whale may be much larger than a vampire bat, but the two mammals behave in similar ways. Both vampire bats and sperm whales hunt in the dark. Vampire bats fly at night. Sperm whales dive deep, where light does not reach.

Both vampire bats and sperm whales find their way by echolocation. When sperm whales dive, they make rapid clicking sounds. The whales listen for the echo of the clicks bouncing off objects. For sperm whales as well as vampire bats, echolocation reveals the location, the size, and the shape of the objects around them.

**DID YOU KNOW?**
Sperm whales can **DIVE** deeper than 3,300 feet (1,000 m) and stay underwater for an hour or two at a time.

Sperm whales also live together in groups, as vampire bats do. Groups of sperm whales are called pods. Females and their offspring swim in one pod. Males travel together with other males or swim alone. Living in groups helps sperm whales find food and fend off predators.

Both vampire bats (*left*) and sperm whales (*right*) live together in groups.

# VAMPIRE BATS VS. GROUNDHOGS

Groundhogs scurry across woods and fields throughout North America. These furry mammals graze on grasses, plants, fruit, and bark. Groundhogs don't just have a different diet from vampire bats. They behave differently from vampire bats too.

Vampire bats live in groups. Groundhogs live alone. Vampire bats avoid sunlight, but groundhogs love it. Not only do groundhogs feed during the day, but they enjoy sunning themselves. At night, when vampire bats hunt, groundhogs doze in underground burrows.

Vampire bats must eat every day. That's not true of groundhogs! They stuff themselves all summer long, growing fatter as the season passes. When winter comes, they head underground and live off their stored fat until spring.

*Groundhogs like to bask in the sun.*

# COMPARE IT!

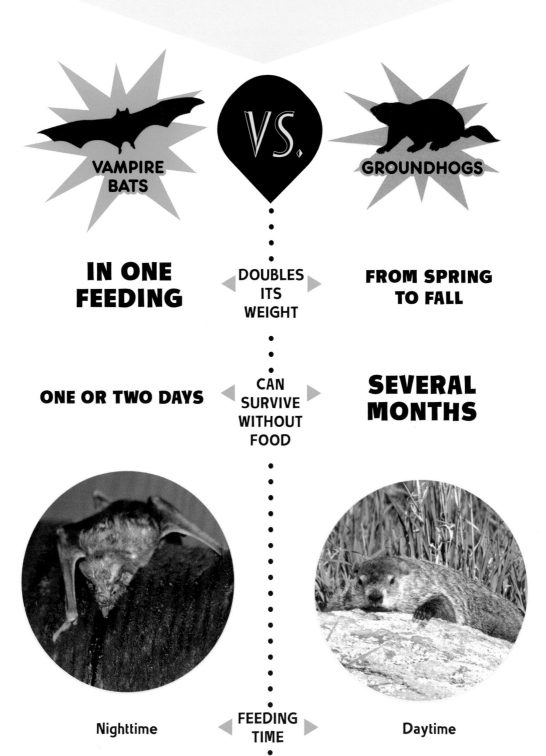

VAMPIRE
BATS

VS.

GROUNDHOGS

IN ONE
FEEDING

◄ DOUBLES
ITS
WEIGHT ►

FROM SPRING
TO FALL

ONE OR TWO DAYS

◄ CAN
SURVIVE
WITHOUT
FOOD ►

SEVERAL
MONTHS

Nighttime

◄ FEEDING
TIME ►

Daytime

# CHAPTER 4

# THE LIFE CYCLE OF VAMPIRE BATS

**Female vampire bats give birth while hanging by their feet.** As a vampire bat pup is born, the mother catches the pup in her wings. Babies are born one at a time, although sometimes mothers give birth to twins. Each newborn is furry and has its eyes open. The pup clings to its mother's fur with its sharp claws.

A vampire bat pup is born with its eyes open.

A vampire bat mother feeds her pup milk for the first two months of the pup's life. In the months that follow, the mother regurgitates blood for the pup. At four months, the pup's wings have developed, and the pup begins to fly with its mother. The pup also learns to hunt.

Two juvenile vampire bats (*center*) hang out with their family.

Vampire bat pups are fully grown in less than a year. The young bats have inherited valuable traits from their parents. They have wings for flying and a taste for blood. These traits will help them survive for about twelve years.

# VAMPIRE BATS VS. GOLDEN LION TAMARINS

Golden lion tamarins run along branches high in the trees of Brazil. These monkeys live in coastal forests. They have thick manes and golden fur. Golden lion tamarins may look different from vampire bats, but these mammals have similar life cycles.

Golden lion tamarin mothers usually give birth to twins. Like vampire bat pups, newborn tamarins come into the world sharing some features with their parents. Newborns are fully furred and have their eyes open. And like a vampire bat pup, a baby tamarin clings to its mother's fur and drinks her milk for the first few months.

As young tamarins begin to eat solid food, adults share their food with the youngsters. This is also true of vampire bats. Golden lion tamarins are able to find their own food at two months. They are fully grown in about two years. Tamarins and vampire bats have similar life spans. Vampire bats live about twelve years. Golden lion tamarins live about fifteen years.

A young golden lion tamarin clings to the back of its mother.

# VAMPIRE BATS VS. MATSCHIE'S TREE KANGAROOS

A Matschie's tree kangaroo peeks through the leaves in a mountain forest in Papua New Guinea. Tree kangaroos climb and hop above the ground. These mammals have different habitats than vampire bats. They also have different life cycles.

A Matschie's tree kangaroo keeps its joey in its pouch.

Matschie's tree kangaroos are marsupials, mammals that have pouches. Marsupials give birth to infants called joeys. The tree kangaroo joey is bald and helpless at birth, unlike the clawed and hairy vampire bat baby. A joey also stays close to its mother longer than a vampire bat pup does. The joey crawls into its mother's pouch and drinks her milk for months while it grows bigger.

# COMPARE IT!

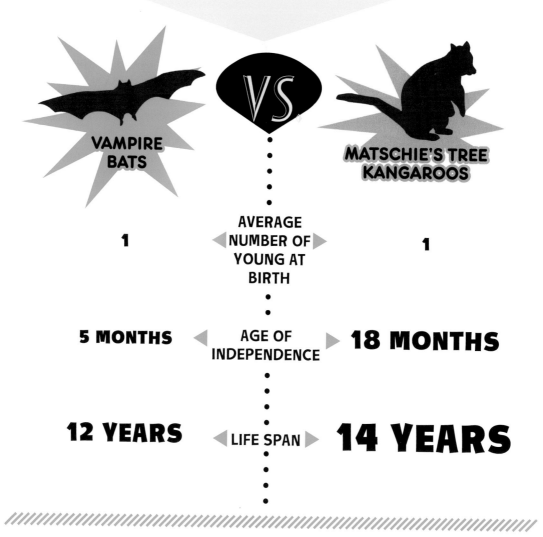

**VAMPIRE BATS**

**VS**

**MATSCHIE'S TREE KANGAROOS**

| | | |
|---|---|---|
| 1 | AVERAGE NUMBER OF YOUNG AT BIRTH | 1 |
| 5 MONTHS | AGE OF INDEPENDENCE | 18 MONTHS |
| 12 YEARS | LIFE SPAN | 14 YEARS |

At eight months old, tree kangaroo joeys first poke their heads out of the pouch. By this stage, vampire bats are fully developed. But joeys are not mature until eighteen months. Although Matschie's tree kangaroos reach adulthood more slowly than vampire bats, they live only a little longer: fourteen years rather than twelve years.

PUBLIC LIBRARY
DANVILLE, ILLINOIS

# VAMPIRE BAT TRAIT CHART

This book explored the way vampire bats are similar to and different from other mammals. What mammals would you add to this list?

| | WARM-BLOODED | HAIR ON BODY | GIVES BIRTH TO LIVE YOUNG | SHARP TEETH | LIVES IN FORESTS | NOCTURNAL |
|---|---|---|---|---|---|---|
| **VAMPIRE BAT** | X | X | X | X | X | X |
| **COLUGO** | X | X | X | | X | X |
| **WALRUS** | X | X | X | X | | |
| **WHITE-LIPPED PECCARY** | X | X | X | X | X | X |
| **POLAR BEAR** | X | X | X | X | | |
| **SPERM WHALE** | X | X | X | X | | |
| **GROUNDHOG** | X | X | X | | X | |
| **GOLDEN LION TAMARIN** | X | X | X | X | X | |
| **MATSCHIE'S TREE KANGAROO** | X | X | X | X | X | |

# GLOSSARY

**adapted:** suited to living in a particular environment

**burrows:** holes in the ground made by an animal for shelter or protection

**forage:** to search an area for food

**habitats:** environments where an animal naturally lives. A habitat is the place where an animal can find food, water, air, shelter, and a place to raise its young.

**host:** a living animal on which another animal depends for survival

**nocturnal:** active at night

**predators:** animals that hunt, or prey on, other animals

**prey:** an animal that is hunted and killed by a predator for food

**regurgitate:** to throw up undigested food

**roost:** to rest or sleep, often in groups

**traits:** features that are inherited from the parents. Body size and fur color are examples of inherited traits.

**warm-blooded:** able to maintain a constant body temperature that is usually warmer than the surrounding environment

**wingspan:** the distance from one tip of one of a pair of wings to the tip of the other wing

LERNER

SOURCE

Expand learning beyond the printed book. Download free, complementary educational resources for this book from our website, www.lerneresource.com.

# SELECTED BIBLIOGRAPHY

"Animal Diversity Web." University of Michigan. May 28, 2014. http://animaldiversity.ummz.umich.edu/accounts/Desmodus_rotundus/.

"Arkive." Wildscreen Arkive. June 7, 2014. http://www.arkive.org/golden-lion-tamarin/leontopithecus-rosalia/.

"Bats." San Diego Zoo. June 7, 2014. http://animals.sandiegozoo.org/animals/bat.

Gould, Edwin, and George McKay. *The Encyclopedia of Mammals*. Sydney: Academic Press, 1998. IUCN 2013. IUCN Red List of Threatened Species. Version 2013.2. June 6, 2014. http://www.iucnredlist.org.

"Mammals." *National Geographic*. June 6, 2014. http://animals.nationalgeographic.com/animals/mammals/groundhog/.

Palca, Joe. "How Bloodsucking Vampire Bats Aim Their Bites." Broadcast on *All Things Considered*. National Public Radio, August 3, 2011. http://www.npr.org/2011/08/03/138953002/how-blood-sucking-vampire-bats-aim-their-bites.

# FURTHER INFORMATION

A-Z Animals: Vampire Bat
http://a-z-animals.com/animals/vampire-bat
Learn more about the lives of vampire bats with this site's photos, map, and Vampire Bat Facts.

Carson, Mary Kay. *The Bat Scientists*. Boston: Houghton Mifflin Books for Children, 2010. Read more about these night-flying predators, how scientists study them, and how people work to save bats from loss of habitat.

Markle, Sandra. *The Case of the Vanishing Little Brown Bats: A Scientific Mystery*. Minneapolis: Millbrook Press, 2015. In this real-life science mystery, follow scientific teams studying why little brown bats are disappearing.

Rodriguez, Ana Maria. *Vampire Bats, Giant Insects, and Other Mysterious Animals of the Darkest Caves*. Berkeley Heights, NJ: Enslow, 2012. Pick up this book to learn more about vampire bats and other remarkable animals that dwell in caves.

# INDEX